I0011981

Table Of Conten ts

Chapter 1: Introduction to IT

Governance in 2024

The Importance of IT Governance

In the rapidly evolving world of technology, the importance of effective IT governance cannot be overstated. As organizations embrace digital transformations and rely more heavily on technology, it is crucial to have a robust framework in place to ensure the efficient and secure management of IT resources. This subchapter explores the significance of IT governance and its implications for various sectors and emerging technologies.

IT governance in 2024 has become even more critical as businesses continue to face new challenges and opportunities. With the increasing complexity of IT systems and the growing reliance on technology, organizations need to establish clear guidelines and processes to ensure that IT investments align with business objectives. CTOs, CEOs, and IT professionals will benefit from understanding the latest strategies and best practices to effectively manage IT resources and enhance decision-making.

AI-powered IT governance is a game-changer in 2024, enabling organizations to leverage the power of artificial intelligence to optimize IT processes, improve efficiency, and reduce costs. By implementing AI-powered governance tools, businesses can automate routine tasks, analyze vast amounts of data, and make data-driven decisions, leading to improved performance and innovation.

IT governance for blockchain technology is another crucial aspect to consider. As blockchain gains traction across industries, organizations must establish governance frameworks to ensure transparency, security, and compliance. Understanding the unique challenges and opportunities presented by blockchain technology will be essential for technology industry leaders and computer science students alike.

Cloud computing has revolutionized the way businesses operate, but it also brings new governance challenges. IT governance for cloud computing involves establishing policies and procedures to ensure data security, privacy, and compliance. CEOs, IT professionals, and information technology students must stay updated on the latest practices and regulations to effectively manage cloud-based resources.

With the rise of the Internet of Things (IoT) devices, organizations face new governance challenges related to data privacy and security. IT governance for IoT devices involves implementing controls to protect sensitive data, manage device proliferation, and ensure compliance with privacy regulations. This subchapter will provide valuable insights for CEOs, IT professionals, and technology industry leaders looking to navigate this rapidly evolving landscape.

In an increasingly interconnected world, cybersecurity and data privacy have become paramount. IT governance for cybersecurity involves establishing frameworks to mitigate risks, implement security controls, and respond to incidents effectively. CEOs, CTOs, and IT professionals must understand the importance of proactive governance to protect their organizations from cyber threats.

The rise of remote and distributed teams has brought new governance challenges. IT governance for remote and distributed teams involves establishing policies and procedures to ensure effective communication, collaboration, and productivity. This subchapter will provide valuable insights for CEOs, IT professionals, and technology industry leaders seeking to optimize remote work environments.

Agile and DevOps methodologies have revolutionized software development and IT operations. However, IT governance for agile and DevOps methodologies requires adapting traditional governance frameworks to accommodate rapid development cycles and continuous delivery. CEOs, CTOs, and computer science students will benefit from understanding the unique governance challenges and best practices associated with these methodologies.

As organizations embark on digital transformation initiatives, IT governance plays a critical role in ensuring their success. IT governance for digital transformation involves aligning IT strategies with business objectives, managing risks, and fostering innovation. CEOs, CTOs, and IT professionals must have a comprehensive understanding of the governance principles and frameworks that drive successful digital transformations.

In conclusion, the importance of IT governance cannot be underestimated in the ever-evolving world of technology. CTOs, CEOs, IT professionals, information technology students, technology industry leaders, and computer science students must stay updated on the latest trends, strategies, and best practices to effectively navigate the complex landscape of IT governance in 2024. Whether it is AI-powered governance, blockchain technology, cloud computing, IoT devices, cybersecurity, remote teams, agile methodologies, or digital transformation, understanding and implementing effective IT governance is essential for success in the digital age.

Overview of IT Governance Trends in 2024

In the rapidly evolving digital landscape, IT governance has become a crucial aspect of organizations' success. As technology continues to advance, CTOs, CEOs, IT professionals, information technology students, technology industry leaders, and computer science students must stay up to date with the latest trends and strategies to ensure effective IT governance. This subchapter provides an overview of the key trends that will shape IT governance in 2024.

One of the most significant trends in IT governance is the integration of artificial intelligence (AI) capabilities. AI-powered IT governance systems leverage machine learning algorithms to automate decision-making processes, enhance risk management, and improve operational efficiency. These systems analyze vast amounts of data in real-time, enabling organizations to make informed decisions and respond quickly to emerging threats and opportunities.

Another emerging trend is IT governance for blockchain technology. With the increasing adoption of blockchain in various industries, organizations need to establish robust governance frameworks to ensure transparency, security, and compliance. Blockchain-based governance systems enable secure and decentralized decision-making, reducing the reliance on centralized authorities while providing an immutable audit trail.

Cloud computing has become an integral part of modern IT infrastructure, and as such, IT governance for cloud computing is gaining prominence. Organizations need to implement governance practices that address data privacy, compliance, and risk management in the cloud environment. Effective governance frameworks ensure that organizations leverage cloud services while maintaining control over their data and ensuring compliance with regulatory requirements.

The Internet of Things (IoT) devices continue to proliferate, connecting various devices and systems. However, the increased connectivity also poses significant governance challenges. IT governance for IoT devices involves managing security risks, ensuring data privacy, and establishing protocols for device management, authentication, and access control.

Cybersecurity and data privacy remain paramount concerns for organizations. IT governance for cybersecurity entails establishing comprehensive security policies, incident response plans, and continuous monitoring systems. Additionally, organizations must adhere to data privacy regulations such as the General Data Protection Regulation (GDPR) and implement privacy-enhancing technologies to protect customer data.

The rise of remote and distributed teams has necessitated a shift in IT governance practices. Organizations need to establish governance frameworks that foster collaboration, communication, and accountability among team members working remotely. This includes implementing secure remote access, robust collaboration tools, and performance measurement mechanisms.

Agile and DevOps methodologies have transformed software development practices, emphasizing speed, flexibility, and continuous improvement. IT governance for agile and DevOps methodologies involves aligning governance practices with these methodologies, ensuring efficient resource allocation, and enabling cross-functional collaboration.

Lastly, IT governance plays a crucial role in driving digital transformation initiatives. Organizations must adopt governance frameworks that facilitate innovation, manage risks, and enable effective decision-making throughout the transformation journey.

In conclusion, IT governance is undergoing significant transformations to adapt to the evolving technological landscape. AI-powered governance systems, blockchain technology, cloud computing, IoT devices, cybersecurity, remote teams, agile methodologies, and digital transformation initiatives are key areas that require effective governance practices. By staying abreast of these trends and implementing appropriate strategies, organizations can ensure successful IT governance in 2024 and beyond.

Key Challenges and Opportunities for IT Governance

In the rapidly evolving landscape of technology, IT governance plays a critical role in enabling organizations to effectively manage their IT resources, mitigate risks, and achieve their strategic goals. However, with the emergence of new technologies and the increasing complexity of IT systems, several key challenges and opportunities arise for IT governance in 2024.

One of the major challenges facing IT governance is the integration of AI-powered technologies. As artificial intelligence continues to advance, organizations are leveraging AI to automate processes, make data-driven decisions, and enhance customer experiences. However, this integration brings forth the challenge of governing the ethical use of AI, ensuring transparency and accountability, and managing the potential bias in AI algorithms. IT governance must adapt to these challenges by establishing robust frameworks and guidelines for the responsible and ethical use of AI.

Another significant challenge is the governance of blockchain technology. As blockchain gains widespread adoption, organizations are exploring its potential to transform various industries, including finance, supply chain, and healthcare. However, the decentralized and distributed nature of blockchain poses challenges in terms of data privacy, security, and regulatory compliance. IT governance must address these challenges by developing frameworks that ensure the secure and compliant implementation of blockchain technology.

Cloud computing is another area where IT governance faces challenges and opportunities. The increasing adoption of cloud services brings benefits such as scalability, flexibility, and cost-efficiency. However, it also raises concerns regarding data security, privacy, and vendor lock-in. IT governance must provide organizations with guidance on selecting trustworthy cloud service providers, implementing robust security measures, and ensuring compliance with data protection regulations.

With the proliferation of Internet of Things (IoT) devices, IT governance must address the challenges of managing and securing these interconnected devices. Organizations need to establish governance mechanisms that ensure the privacy and security of IoT data, while also leveraging the insights derived from IoT devices to make informed business decisions.

Cybersecurity and data privacy continue to be critical concerns for organizations in 2024. IT governance must focus on establishing comprehensive security frameworks, implementing effective risk management strategies, and ensuring compliance with data protection regulations. Additionally, IT governance should address the challenges of managing remote and distributed teams, as organizations increasingly embrace remote work arrangements. This requires implementing robust governance mechanisms to ensure effective communication, collaboration, and cybersecurity in remote work environments.

Furthermore, IT governance must adapt to the agile and DevOps methodologies that have gained popularity in software development. Organizations are embracing these methodologies to increase speed, flexibility, and collaboration in software development. IT governance must provide guidelines on integrating agile and DevOps practices into existing governance frameworks, ensuring alignment with organizational goals and effective risk management.

Lastly, IT governance plays a crucial role in supporting digital transformation initiatives. As organizations undergo digital transformation, IT governance must provide guidance on aligning IT strategies with business objectives, managing the digital skills gap, and ensuring the successful implementation of digital initiatives.

In conclusion, the future of IT governance in 2024 presents both challenges and opportunities. By addressing the key challenges of AI-powered technologies, blockchain, cloud computing, IoT devices, cybersecurity, remote teams, agile and DevOps methodologies, and digital transformation, IT governance can enable organizations to navigate the evolving technology landscape effectively and achieve their strategic goals.

Chapter 2: AI-powered IT Governance

Understanding AI-powered IT Governance

In today's rapidly evolving technological landscape, IT governance plays a critical role in ensuring the effective and secure management of information technology resources within organizations. With the continuous advancements in artificial intelligence (AI), a new era of IT governance has emerged – AI-powered IT governance. This subchapter aims to provide an in-depth understanding of this innovative approach to IT governance and its implications for the future.

AI-powered IT governance leverages the capabilities of AI technologies to automate and enhance decision-making processes, improve efficiency, and enable proactive risk management. By utilizing machine learning algorithms and data analytics, organizations can analyze vast amounts of data in real-time, identify patterns, and make informed decisions based on predictive insights. This not only streamlines IT governance processes but also enables organizations to stay ahead of potential risks and vulnerabilities.

One area where AI-powered IT governance is particularly relevant is in the management of emerging technologies such as blockchain, cloud computing, and Internet of Things (IoT) devices. These technologies bring unique governance challenges due to their complexity and scale. AI-powered IT governance can provide organizations with the tools and frameworks to effectively monitor, control, and secure these technologies, ensuring their successful integration into existing IT infrastructure.

Furthermore, AI-powered IT governance also addresses the growing concerns surrounding cybersecurity and data privacy. With the increasing frequency and sophistication of cyber threats, organizations need robust governance frameworks that can adapt and respond to evolving risks. AI-powered technologies can continuously monitor network traffic, detect anomalies, and autonomously respond to potential threats, significantly enhancing cybersecurity measures.

In addition, AI-powered IT governance is also well-suited for managing remote and distributed teams, as well as agile and DevOps methodologies. With the rise of remote work and agile practices, traditional governance models often struggle to keep pace with the speed and flexibility demanded by these approaches. AI-powered technologies can automate project management tasks, facilitate collaboration, and provide real-time insights, enabling organizations to effectively govern distributed teams and agile projects.

Finally, AI-powered IT governance is a crucial enabler of digital transformation initiatives. As organizations undergo digital transformations, they need robust governance frameworks to ensure the successful implementation of new technologies, processes, and business models. AI-powered technologies can help organizations identify areas for improvement, optimize processes, and drive innovation, ultimately ensuring the success of digital transformation initiatives.

In conclusion, AI-powered IT governance represents a paradigm shift in how organizations manage and govern their IT resources. By harnessing the power of AI technologies, organizations can enhance decision-making, improve efficiency, and effectively navigate the ever-evolving technological landscape. This subchapter provides valuable insights and strategies for CTOs, CEOs, IT professionals, technology industry leaders, and students, enabling them to embrace the potential of AI-powered IT governance and drive success in their respective domains.

Benefits and Potential Risks of AI-powered IT Governance

In recent years, Artificial Intelligence (AI) has revolutionized various industries, and the field of IT governance is no exception. AI-powered IT governance has emerged as a game-changer, offering numerous benefits and opportunities for organizations to streamline their operations, enhance decision-making processes, and improve overall efficiency. However, it is essential to understand both the benefits and potential risks associated with this technology to make informed decisions and mitigate any potential drawbacks.

One of the significant benefits of AI-powered IT governance is its ability to automate routine tasks and processes. AI algorithms can analyze vast volumes of data, identify patterns, and make predictions, reducing the manual effort required by IT professionals. This automation allows IT teams to focus on more strategic initiatives, such as developing innovative solutions and driving digital transformation.

Furthermore, AI-powered IT governance enhances decision-making processes by providing real-time insights and actionable recommendations. By leveraging advanced analytics and machine learning, organizations can gain valuable insights into their IT infrastructure, identify potential risks or bottlenecks, and proactively address them. This proactive approach enables CTOs and IT professionals to make data-driven decisions that align with business objectives and drive growth.

Another significant benefit of AI-powered IT governance is its ability to enhance cybersecurity and data privacy. AI algorithms can detect and respond to potential cyber threats in real-time, minimizing the risk of data breaches or security incidents. Additionally, AI can assist in ensuring compliance with regulatory requirements by continuously monitoring and analyzing data privacy practices, reducing the likelihood of non-compliance penalties.

However, it is crucial to acknowledge the potential risks associated with AI-powered IT governance. One major concern is the ethical implications of relying heavily on AI algorithms. These algorithms are only as good as the data they are trained on, and biased or incomplete data can lead to skewed results or discriminatory decision-making. Therefore, organizations must ensure transparency, fairness, and accountability when implementing AI-powered IT governance.

Moreover, the reliance on AI raises concerns about job displacement. As routine tasks become automated, some IT professionals may find their roles redundant. However, organizations can mitigate this risk by upskilling and reskilling their workforce to adapt to the changing landscape and focus on higher-value activities that require human expertise.

In conclusion, AI-powered IT governance offers numerous benefits, including automation of routine tasks, enhanced decision-making, improved cybersecurity, and data privacy. However, organizations must be mindful of potential risks, such as biased decision-making and job displacement. By understanding and addressing these risks, CTOs, CEOs, IT professionals, and students can leverage AI-powered IT governance to drive successful IT governance strategies in various domains, including blockchain technology, cloud computing, Internet of Things (IoT) devices, cybersecurity, remote and distributed teams, agile and DevOps methodologies, and digital transformation initiatives.

Implementing AI in IT Governance Processes

In today's rapidly evolving technological landscape, the integration of artificial intelligence (AI) has become a vital component of effective IT governance processes. As we look ahead to 2024, AI-powered IT governance holds immense potential to revolutionize the way organizations manage and optimize their IT infrastructure. This subchapter explores the various applications of AI in different domains of IT governance and highlights its significance in driving success in the digital era.

One of the key areas where AI can make a significant impact is in IT governance for blockchain technology. As blockchain gains wider adoption across industries, organizations face the challenge of ensuring secure and efficient management of blockchain networks. AI can enhance the governance of blockchain systems by automating key tasks such as smart contract monitoring, anomaly detection, and consensus algorithm optimization. By leveraging AI, CTOs and IT professionals can streamline the governance processes associated with blockchain technology, ensuring its reliable and secure operation.

Another domain where AI-powered IT governance can drive significant value is in cloud computing. As the reliance on cloud services continues to grow, organizations need effective governance mechanisms to manage cloud resources, ensure data security, and optimize costs. AI algorithms can analyze large volumes of data generated by cloud platforms, enabling CTOs and IT leaders to make data-driven decisions regarding resource allocation, performance optimization, and security enhancements. This AI-driven approach to cloud governance can enhance operational efficiency, reduce costs, and mitigate risks associated with cloud-based services.

The Internet of Things (IoT) devices present another area where AI can play a crucial role in IT governance. With the proliferation of IoT devices, organizations face the challenge of managing and securing the vast amount of data generated by these devices. AI algorithms can analyze and interpret IoT data in real-time, enabling organizations to detect anomalies, predict failures, and optimize performance. By implementing AI-powered IT governance for IoT devices, CTOs can ensure the reliability, security, and efficiency of their IoT infrastructure.

In the realm of cybersecurity and data privacy, AI can be a game-changer. With the rise in sophisticated cyber threats, organizations need robust governance processes to protect their sensitive data. AI can enhance cybersecurity governance by automating threat detection, incident response, and vulnerability management. By leveraging AI-powered solutions, CTOs and IT professionals can proactively identify and mitigate cybersecurity risks, ensuring data privacy and maintaining business continuity.

Furthermore, as organizations increasingly adopt remote and distributed work models, implementing effective IT governance becomes crucial. AI can assist in monitoring and managing remote teams by analyzing productivity data, identifying bottlenecks, and providing insights for process optimization. This AI-driven governance approach enables organizations to maintain accountability, collaboration, and performance in remote work environments.

Moreover, AI can enhance IT governance for agile and DevOps methodologies. By harnessing AI algorithms, CTOs and IT leaders can automate the planning, monitoring, and optimization of agile and DevOps projects. AI-powered tools can analyze project data, identify areas for improvement, and provide real-time insights to enhance project management and delivery.

Lastly, AI can be instrumental in driving successful digital transformation initiatives. By leveraging AI-powered analytics, organizations can gain valuable insights into customer behavior, market trends, and business operations. This data-driven approach to IT governance enables organizations to make informed decisions, adapt quickly to changing market dynamics, and achieve their digital transformation goals.

In conclusion, the integration of AI in IT governance processes is essential for organizations to thrive in the digital era. From blockchain technology to cloud computing, IoT devices to cybersecurity, remote teams to agile methodologies, and digital transformation initiatives, AI holds the key to optimizing IT governance across various domains. CTOs, CEOs, IT professionals, information technology students, technology industry leaders, and computer science students must embrace AI-powered IT governance to stay ahead in the dynamic and competitive landscape of 2024.

Chapter 3: IT Governance for Blockchain Technology

Introduction to Blockchain Technology

Blockchain technology has emerged as one of the most disruptive and transformative innovations of the 21st century. Its potential impact on various industries and sectors has captured the attention of CTOs, CEOs, IT professionals, information technology students, technology industry leaders, and computer science students alike. In this subchapter, we will delve into the basics of blockchain technology and its role in the future of IT governance.

At its core, blockchain is a decentralized and distributed ledger that records transactions across multiple computers or nodes. Unlike traditional centralized systems, blockchain offers transparency, security, immutability, and trust through its consensus mechanisms. This technology has gained prominence primarily due to its association with cryptocurrencies like Bitcoin. However, its applications extend far beyond digital currencies.

Blockchain technology has the potential to revolutionize IT governance in various domains. In 2024, AI-powered IT governance will become increasingly prevalent, and blockchain can enhance this by providing a secure and transparent platform for managing and auditing AI algorithms and decision-making processes. Additionally, blockchain can play a crucial role in ensuring the integrity and security of IT governance for cloud computing, Internet of Things (IoT) devices, cybersecurity, data privacy, and remote and distributed teams.

Furthermore, as organizations increasingly adopt agile and DevOps methodologies to drive digital transformation initiatives, blockchain can provide a decentralized and secure framework for managing and tracking software development processes. Its transparent and immutable nature can enhance accountability, traceability, and auditability, thereby improving IT governance practices.

Understanding the fundamentals of blockchain technology is essential for IT professionals and students, as it represents a paradigm shift in how data and transactions are managed. This subchapter will explore the key concepts of blockchain, including distributed consensus mechanisms, cryptographic principles, smart contracts, and the different types of blockchains (public, private, and consortium). Moreover, it will highlight real-world use cases and success stories across industries, such as supply chain management, healthcare, finance, and voting systems.

In conclusion, the introduction to blockchain technology in this subchapter serves as a gateway to understanding its potential impact on the future of IT governance. By embracing this technology, CTOs, CEOs, IT professionals, and students can gain a competitive edge, drive innovation, and navigate the complex IT landscape of 2024 and beyond.

Incorporating Blockchain in IT Governance Frameworks

As we look ahead to the future of IT governance in 2024, it is clear that emerging technologies will play a pivotal role in shaping the landscape. One such technology that has gained significant attention and potential is blockchain. This subchapter explores the importance of incorporating blockchain in IT governance frameworks and how it can drive success for organizations across various sectors.

Blockchain, often associated with cryptocurrencies like Bitcoin, is a decentralized and transparent ledger system. Its unique properties of immutability, security, and trust make it an ideal candidate for enhancing IT governance practices. By incorporating blockchain into existing governance frameworks, organizations can benefit from increased transparency, accountability, and efficiency.

CTOs, CEOs, IT professionals, and industry leaders need to understand the potential of blockchain in IT governance. As blockchain technology gains wider adoption, organizations must adapt their governance frameworks to ensure its seamless integration. This subchapter will provide insights into the strategies and best practices required to successfully incorporate blockchain in IT governance frameworks.

For IT professionals and computer science students, understanding the intricacies of blockchain in IT governance will be crucial for their future career growth. This subchapter will delve into the technical aspects of blockchain and its impact on IT governance, equipping them with the knowledge and skills needed to navigate the evolving landscape.

Additionally, this subchapter will explore how blockchain can revolutionize IT governance for various emerging technologies. It will cover AI-powered IT governance, cloud computing, Internet of Things (IoT) devices, cybersecurity and data privacy, remote and distributed teams, agile and DevOps methodologies, and digital transformation initiatives. Each of these niches poses unique challenges and opportunities for IT governance, and blockchain can provide innovative solutions.

The Future of IT Governance in 2024: Strategies for Success is a comprehensive guide addressing the evolving landscape of IT governance. This subchapter on incorporating blockchain in IT governance frameworks will serve as a roadmap for CTOs, CEOs, IT professionals, and industry leaders looking to harness the power of blockchain technology. It will also provide valuable insights for information technology and computer science students, preparing them for the future of IT governance.

In conclusion, incorporating blockchain in IT governance frameworks is essential for organizations aiming to stay ahead in the rapidly evolving technological landscape. This subchapter will provide a comprehensive analysis of the potential of blockchain in IT governance, offering practical strategies and insights for success.

Ensuring Security and Compliance in Blockchain-based IT Governance

In today's rapidly evolving technological landscape, blockchain technology has emerged as a game-changer in various industries. Its decentralized nature and cryptographic security have made it an ideal solution for IT governance. However, as with any disruptive technology, ensuring security and compliance in blockchain-based IT governance is of paramount importance. This subchapter explores the strategies and best practices for maintaining a robust and secure IT governance framework in the blockchain era.

One of the key challenges in blockchain-based IT governance is maintaining data integrity and confidentiality. Blockchain technology relies on consensus algorithms and cryptographic techniques to ensure the immutability and security of data. However, it is crucial to implement additional security measures to protect sensitive information from unauthorized access. This can be achieved through the use of encryption, multi-factor authentication, and secure key management systems.

Compliance with regulatory requirements is another critical aspect of blockchain-based IT governance. As blockchain technology operates across multiple jurisdictions, it is essential to navigate the complex landscape of legal and regulatory frameworks. Organizations must actively engage with regulators and stay abreast of evolving compliance standards to ensure their blockchain-based IT governance practices remain compliant.

Furthermore, organizations must address the unique security challenges associated with blockchain technology. Smart contracts, which are self-executing contracts with the terms of the agreement directly written into code, introduce potential vulnerabilities. To mitigate these risks, organizations should conduct rigorous code reviews, implement bug bounties, and continuously monitor and update smart contracts to protect against potential exploits.

In addition to security and compliance, organizations must also consider the scalability and performance of blockchain-based IT governance systems. As blockchain networks grow in size and complexity, scalability becomes a crucial factor. Implementing sharding techniques, off-chain solutions, and optimizing consensus algorithms can help overcome scalability challenges and ensure smooth operations.

To conclude, ensuring security and compliance in blockchain-based IT governance is a multifaceted task. Organizations need to adopt a proactive approach by implementing robust security measures, staying compliant with regulations, addressing unique blockchain security challenges, and optimizing performance and scalability. By doing so, CTOs, CEOs, IT professionals, and technology industry leaders can confidently embrace blockchain technology in their IT governance strategies, leading to successful digital transformation initiatives in 2024 and beyond.

Chapter 4: IT Governance for Cloud Computing

Overview of Cloud Computing in 2024

Cloud computing has become an integral part of the technological landscape in recent years, and its significance is only expected to grow in the coming years. As we look ahead to 2024, it is essential for CTOs, CEOs, IT professionals, information technology students, technology industry leaders, and computer science students to have a comprehensive understanding of cloud computing and its role in IT governance.

Cloud computing refers to the delivery of computing services, including storage, servers, databases, software, and networking, over the internet. It offers numerous benefits such as scalability, flexibility, cost efficiency, and enhanced collaboration, making it an attractive option for organizations of all sizes and industries.

In 2024, cloud computing will continue to evolve and transform IT governance practices. AI-powered IT governance will leverage the capabilities of artificial intelligence and machine learning algorithms to analyze vast amounts of data, identify patterns, and make informed decisions. This will enable organizations to optimize their cloud infrastructure, improve security measures, and streamline operations.

Furthermore, IT governance for blockchain technology will gain prominence as more industries adopt this revolutionary technology. Cloud computing will play a crucial role in supporting blockchain networks, ensuring their scalability, performance, and security.

The proliferation of Internet of Things (IoT) devices will also drive the need for effective IT governance. Cloud computing will provide the necessary infrastructure to manage and process the massive amounts of data generated by these devices, enabling organizations to leverage IoT capabilities securely and efficiently.

In the realm of cybersecurity and data privacy, cloud computing will play a vital role in enhancing IT governance practices. Cloud-based security solutions will enable organizations to protect their data from ever-evolving threats, while also ensuring compliance with data privacy regulations.

Additionally, as remote and distributed teams become more prevalent, cloud computing will facilitate effective IT governance for these teams. Cloud-based collaboration tools and platforms will enable seamless communication and collaboration, regardless of geographical locations.

Agile and DevOps methodologies will continue to gain traction in 2024, and cloud computing will provide the necessary infrastructure and resources to support these practices. The scalability and flexibility of cloud computing will enable organizations to rapidly deploy and test new applications and services, fostering innovation and agility.

Finally, cloud computing will be a critical enabler for digital transformation initiatives. Organizations will leverage cloud-based technologies and services to modernize their IT infrastructure, enhance customer experiences, and drive business growth.

In conclusion, cloud computing will play a pivotal role in the future of IT governance in 2024. From AI-powered IT governance to support for blockchain technology, IoT devices, cybersecurity, remote teams, agile methodologies, and digital transformation initiatives, cloud computing will be at the forefront of enabling organizations to thrive in the rapidly evolving technological landscape. It is imperative for CTOs, CEOs, IT professionals, information technology students, technology industry leaders, and computer science students to stay informed and embrace the potential of cloud computing in their organizations.

Integrating Cloud Computing in IT Governance Strategies

Cloud computing has emerged as a game-changing technology that has revolutionized the way businesses operate. It offers unparalleled flexibility, scalability, and cost-effectiveness, making it an essential component of any modern IT infrastructure. As organizations increasingly adopt cloud computing, it is crucial to integrate it into their IT governance strategies to ensure seamless operations and maximize its benefits.

In the book "The Future of IT Governance in 2024: Strategies for Success," we explore the significance of integrating cloud computing into IT governance strategies for various stakeholders, including CTOs, CEOs, IT professionals, information technology students, technology industry leaders, and computer science students. We delve into the niches of IT governance in 2024, AI-powered IT governance, IT governance for blockchain technology, IT governance for cloud computing, IT governance for Internet of Things (IoT) devices, IT governance for cybersecurity and data privacy, IT governance for remote and distributed teams, IT governance for agile and DevOps methodologies, and IT governance for digital transformation initiatives.

Cloud computing offers numerous advantages, such as increased agility, accessibility, and scalability. However, its integration into IT governance strategies requires careful planning and implementation. One of the key aspects to consider is the alignment of cloud computing with business objectives and IT governance frameworks. This ensures that cloud services are utilized in a manner that supports the organization's goals while adhering to regulatory and compliance requirements.

Furthermore, the integration of cloud computing in IT governance strategies necessitates addressing security and privacy concerns. As cloud environments are shared and inherently vulnerable to cyber threats, robust security measures must be implemented to safeguard sensitive data. This includes data encryption, access controls, regular audits, and monitoring.

Another crucial consideration is the management of cloud service providers. Organizations must establish clear guidelines and processes for selecting and managing cloud vendors. This involves assessing their reliability, performance, and adherence to security standards.

Additionally, organizations need to establish comprehensive service-level agreements (SLAs) to ensure that the cloud services meet their specific requirements and expectations.

Moreover, integrating cloud computing in IT governance strategies requires a shift in IT management practices. Traditional IT governance models may need to be adapted to accommodate the unique characteristics and challenges of cloud computing. This includes redefining roles and responsibilities, revisiting policies and procedures, and implementing effective monitoring and control mechanisms.

In conclusion, the integration of cloud computing in IT governance strategies is essential for organizations seeking to capitalize on its benefits. This subchapter provides valuable insights into the significance of this integration for various stakeholders, including CTOs, CEOs, IT professionals, information technology students, technology industry leaders, and computer science students. By effectively integrating cloud computing into IT governance strategies, organizations can drive innovation, enhance operational efficiencies, and ensure a competitive edge in the rapidly evolving digital landscape.

Addressing Security and Privacy Concerns in Cloud-based IT Governance

In the rapidly evolving digital landscape of 2024, cloud-based IT governance has become an integral part of organizations' overall IT strategies. As CTOs, CEOs, IT professionals, Information Technology students, Technology industry leaders, and computer science students, it is crucial to understand the security and privacy concerns associated with this emerging technology.

Cloud computing offers numerous benefits, such as cost savings, scalability, and flexibility. However, it also introduces new challenges, particularly in the areas of security and privacy. Organizations must prioritize addressing these concerns to ensure the safe and efficient use of cloud-based IT governance.

One of the primary security concerns in cloud-based IT governance is data breaches. As more sensitive and confidential information is stored and processed in the cloud, the risk of unauthorized access and data theft increases. Organizations must implement robust encryption techniques, access controls, and authentication mechanisms to protect their data from malicious actors.

Privacy is another critical concern in the cloud environment. Organizations must comply with data protection regulations and ensure that personally identifiable information (PII) is handled securely. Implementing privacy-enhancing technologies, such as data anonymization and pseudonymization, can help mitigate the risk of privacy breaches.

To address these security and privacy concerns, organizations can adopt various strategies. Firstly, conducting thorough risk assessments and audits can identify potential vulnerabilities and weaknesses in the cloud infrastructure. Regular security testing and penetration testing can provide valuable insights into the system's security posture.

Secondly, organizations should prioritize selecting reputable and trustworthy cloud service providers. Evaluating their security measures, certifications, and compliance with industry standards can help ensure the integrity of the cloud environment.

Additionally, implementing a comprehensive security and privacy policy is crucial. This policy should outline the organization's guidelines, procedures, and responsibilities concerning security and privacy in the cloud environment. Regular training and awareness programs can educate employees about best practices and potential threats.

In conclusion, as cloud-based IT governance continues to gain prominence in 2024, addressing security and privacy concerns becomes paramount. CTOs, CEOs, IT professionals, Information Technology students, Technology industry leaders, and computer science students must understand the risks associated with cloud computing and implement robust measures to mitigate these risks. By prioritizing data protection, complying with regulations, and adopting best practices, organizations can embrace cloud-based IT governance securely and confidently.

Chapter 5: IT Governance for Internet of Things (IoT) Devices

The Rise of IoT in 2024

The year 2024 marks a significant milestone in the world of technology as the Internet of Things (IoT) takes center stage. With IoT devices becoming an integral part of our daily lives, businesses and organizations are embracing this technology to enhance their operations, improve efficiency, and unlock new opportunities. In this subchapter, we will explore the rise of IoT in 2024 and its implications for various aspects of IT governance.

For CTOs, CEOs, and IT professionals, understanding the impact of IoT on IT governance is crucial for staying ahead in the rapidly evolving technological landscape. AI-powered IT governance will play a pivotal role in managing the vast amount of data generated by IoT devices. Machine learning algorithms will analyze this data to identify patterns, detect anomalies, and make informed decisions to optimize IT operations.

Furthermore, IT governance for blockchain technology will become increasingly important as organizations leverage the decentralized nature of blockchain to secure IoT transactions and ensure data integrity. This technology will enable seamless and secure communication between IoT devices, creating a trustless environment for businesses.

Cloud computing will continue to be a key component of IT infrastructure, and IT governance for cloud computing will need to adapt to the growing number of IoT devices connected to the cloud. Robust governance frameworks will be required to manage the scalability, security, and privacy concerns associated with IoT data in the cloud.

The proliferation of IoT devices also presents significant cybersecurity and data privacy challenges. IT governance for cybersecurity and data privacy will focus on implementing robust security measures, ensuring compliance with privacy regulations, and developing incident response plans to mitigate the risks associated with IoT devices.

In addition, IT governance for remote and distributed teams will become increasingly important as IoT devices enable employees to work from anywhere. This will require organizations to establish policies and procedures to effectively manage and secure IoT devices used by remote teams.

Agile and DevOps methodologies will continue to gain traction in 2024, and IT governance for agile and DevOps methodologies will need to integrate IoT devices seamlessly into development and deployment processes. This will require close collaboration between IT and other departments to ensure that IoT projects align with business objectives and are developed and deployed efficiently.

Finally, IT governance for digital transformation initiatives will incorporate IoT as a key enabler of organizational change. This will involve reimagining business processes, leveraging IoT data to drive innovation, and developing strategies to harness the full potential of IoT in driving digital transformation.

In conclusion, the rise of IoT in 2024 will have a profound impact on IT governance. CTOs, CEOs, IT professionals, and students must adapt to this paradigm shift by understanding the implications of IoT for various aspects of IT governance such as AI-powered IT governance, blockchain technology, cloud computing, cybersecurity and data privacy, remote and distributed teams, agile and DevOps methodologies, and digital transformation initiatives. By embracing IoT and effectively managing its governance, organizations can unlock new opportunities, enhance their operations, and stay ahead in the rapidly evolving technological landscape.

Managing IT Governance for IoT Devices

In the fast-paced world of technology, the Internet of Things (IoT) has emerged as a transformative force, connecting billions of devices and generating vast amounts of data. With this growth comes the need for effective management of IT governance for IoT devices. In this subchapter, we will explore the strategies and best practices for successfully managing IT governance for IoT devices in the year 2024.

CTOs, CEOs, IT professionals, information technology students, technology industry leaders, computer science students, and anyone interested in the future of IT governance in 2024 will find this subchapter informative and valuable. We will delve into the various aspects of IT governance, including AI-powered IT governance, IT governance for blockchain technology, IT governance for cloud computing, and IT governance for cybersecurity and data privacy.

One of the key challenges in managing IT governance for IoT devices is the sheer scale and complexity of the IoT ecosystem. With billions of interconnected devices, ensuring security, data privacy, and compliance becomes paramount. We will discuss the importance of implementing robust cybersecurity measures and data privacy policies to protect sensitive information and mitigate risks.

Furthermore, we will explore the role of AI-powered IT governance in managing the complexities of IoT devices. AI can be leveraged to automate and optimize IT governance processes, enabling organizations to monitor and manage their IoT devices more efficiently. We will discuss the potential benefits and challenges of implementing AI-powered IT governance in the context of IoT devices.

Additionally, as remote and distributed teams become more prevalent, we will examine the implications of IT governance for such teams. We will discuss how to effectively manage IT governance for remote and distributed teams, ensuring collaboration, communication, and adherence to governance policies.

Furthermore, with the rise of agile and DevOps methodologies, we will explore how IT governance can adapt to support these approaches. We will discuss the challenges and opportunities of integrating IT governance into agile and DevOps methodologies, ensuring alignment between development teams and governance practices.

Finally, we will discuss the role of IT governance in driving digital transformation initiatives. As organizations strive to innovate and adopt new technologies, IT governance becomes even more critical. We will explore how IT governance can support and enable digital transformation initiatives, ensuring successful outcomes.

In conclusion, managing IT governance for IoT devices is a complex and evolving challenge. This subchapter will provide valuable insights and practical strategies for CTOs,

CEOs, IT professionals, information technology students, and technology industry leaders to navigate the ever-changing landscape of IT governance in the year 2024. By understanding and implementing effective IT governance practices, organizations can harness the full potential of IoT devices while ensuring security, compliance, and successful digital transformation.

Ensuring Security and Privacy in IoT-based IT Governance

In today's rapidly evolving digital landscape, the Internet of Things (IoT) has emerged as a transformative force, revolutionizing the way businesses operate and interact with their customers. However, with the increasing adoption of IoT devices in various industries, ensuring security and privacy has become paramount for effective IT governance. This subchapter explores the challenges and strategies for safeguarding sensitive data and maintaining privacy in an IoT-based IT governance environment.

For CTOs, CEOs, IT professionals, and technology industry leaders, understanding the potential risks associated with IoT devices is crucial. As these devices collect and transmit large amounts of sensitive data, they become attractive targets for cybercriminals. To mitigate these risks, organizations should implement robust security measures, including encryption protocols, secure authentication mechanisms, and regular vulnerability assessments. Additionally, adopting a proactive approach to security, such as conducting penetration testing and continuously monitoring IoT devices, can help identify and address vulnerabilities before they are exploited.

Information technology students and computer science students interested in IT governance in 2024 will benefit from understanding the unique challenges posed by IoT devices. They should be aware of the potential privacy concerns surrounding the collection and usage of personal data by these devices. Organizations must adopt privacy-by-design principles, ensuring that data protection is embedded into the design and development of IoT devices.

Implementing user consent mechanisms, data anonymization techniques, and strict data retention policies can help organizations strike a balance between utilizing data for innovation and respecting individual privacy rights.

Furthermore, the subchapter will address the specific IT governance considerations for AI-powered IT governance, blockchain technology, cloud computing, cybersecurity, data privacy, remote and distributed teams, agile and DevOps methodologies, and digital transformation initiatives. Each of these niches presents its own unique challenges and opportunities for ensuring security and privacy in an IoT-based IT governance environment. By exploring best practices and case studies in each of these domains, IT professionals can gain valuable insights into how to effectively integrate IoT devices into their organizations' governance frameworks.

In conclusion, ensuring security and privacy in an IoT-based IT governance environment is essential for organizations to leverage the full potential of IoT devices while safeguarding sensitive data. By adopting robust security measures, privacy-by-design principles, and staying updated on the evolving IoT landscape, organizations can effectively address the challenges posed by IoT devices and create a secure and privacy-centric IT governance framework.

Chapter 6: IT Governance for

Cybersecurity and Data Privacy

Understanding the Importance of Cybersecurity and Data Privacy

In today's digital age, where technology is advancing at an unprecedented pace, cybersecurity and data privacy have become critical concerns for individuals, businesses, and governments alike. The rapid growth of interconnected systems and the increasing reliance on digital platforms have exposed us to a myriad of cyber threats and vulnerabilities. As a result, understanding the importance of cybersecurity and data privacy has become an essential skill for CTOs, CEOs, IT professionals, information technology students, technology industry leaders, computer science students, and anyone involved in IT governance in 2024.

With the advent of AI-powered IT governance, blockchain technology, cloud computing, Internet of Things (IoT) devices, cybersecurity and data privacy have taken center stage. These emerging technologies have transformed the way businesses operate, creating new opportunities, but also new risks. As a CTO or IT professional, it is crucial to comprehend how cybersecurity and data privacy intersect with these technologies and how they can impact your organization's overall IT governance strategy.

Cybersecurity threats such as data breaches, ransomware attacks, and identity theft can have severe consequences for businesses, including financial loss, reputational damage, and legal implications. Therefore, implementing robust cybersecurity measures and ensuring data privacy should be a top priority for all organizations, regardless of their size or industry.

Moreover, IT governance for remote and distributed teams has become increasingly relevant in today's globalized and interconnected world. With the rise of remote work and distributed teams, ensuring the security and privacy of sensitive data across different locations and devices has become a complex challenge. Understanding how to effectively govern these remote teams and enforce cybersecurity protocols is crucial for maintaining a secure working environment.

Furthermore, IT governance for agile and DevOps methodologies is essential for organizations looking to embrace digital transformation initiatives. Agile and DevOps methodologies enable rapid development and deployment of software, but they also introduce new risks. It is vital to establish proper security controls and integrate cybersecurity and data privacy into the development lifecycle to mitigate these risks effectively.

In conclusion, understanding the importance of cybersecurity and data privacy is paramount in today's technology-driven world. Whether you are a CTO, CEO, IT professional, information technology student, technology industry leader, or computer science student, being well-versed in these topics is essential for successful IT governance in 2024. By prioritizing cybersecurity and data privacy, organizations can protect their assets, ensure regulatory compliance, and foster trust among their stakeholders.

Incorporating Cybersecurity Measures in IT Governance

As technology continues to evolve at an unprecedented pace, the importance of cybersecurity measures in IT governance cannot be overstated. With the rise of AI-powered IT governance, blockchain technology, cloud computing, Internet of Things (IoT) devices, cybersecurity and data privacy concerns, remote and distributed teams, agile and DevOps methodologies, and digital transformation initiatives, organizations must prioritize the integration of robust cybersecurity measures into their IT governance frameworks.

For CTOs, CEOs, and IT professionals, understanding the significance of incorporating cybersecurity measures in IT governance is crucial in ensuring the security and integrity of their organization's digital assets. Cybersecurity threats are constantly evolving, and without proper measures in place, businesses are vulnerable to data breaches, ransomware attacks, and other cybersecurity incidents that can have devastating consequences. By incorporating cybersecurity into their IT governance strategies, organizations can proactively identify and mitigate potential vulnerabilities, safeguard sensitive data, and protect their reputation.

Information technology students and computer science students can greatly benefit from gaining knowledge and understanding of the importance of cybersecurity measures in IT governance. As they enter the workforce, they will be equipped with the necessary skills to develop and implement robust cybersecurity strategies. Furthermore, they will be able to contribute to the development of AI-powered IT governance systems and blockchain technology that prioritize security and privacy.

Technology industry leaders have a responsibility to lead by example and champion the integration of cybersecurity measures in IT governance. By doing so, they not only protect their own organizations but also set a precedent for others to follow. As the industry continues to evolve, it is crucial for technology leaders to stay informed about the latest cybersecurity trends and best practices, ensuring that their organizations remain at the forefront of cybersecurity innovation.

In conclusion, incorporating cybersecurity measures in IT governance is essential in today's rapidly evolving technological landscape. Whether it is AI-powered IT governance, blockchain technology, cloud computing, IoT devices, cybersecurity and data privacy concerns, remote and distributed teams, agile and DevOps methodologies, or digital transformation initiatives, organizations must prioritize cybersecurity to protect their digital assets and maintain the trust of their stakeholders. By doing so, they can confidently navigate the challenges of the future and ensure the success and sustainability of their businesses.

Addressing Data Privacy Regulations in IT Governance

In today's digital age, data privacy has become a critical concern for organizations across industries. With the increasing number of data breaches and cyber threats, it has become imperative for businesses to address data privacy regulations in their IT governance strategies. This subchapter will explore the importance of data privacy regulations in the context of IT governance and provide strategies for ensuring compliance in the year 2024.

CTOs, CEOs, IT professionals, information technology students, technology industry leaders, and computer science students will find this subchapter particularly valuable as it addresses the emerging challenges and opportunities in IT governance in the year 2024. By understanding the significance of data privacy regulations, these individuals can develop effective strategies to protect their organizations' data and ensure compliance with the evolving regulatory landscape.

The subchapter will cover various niches within IT governance, including AI-powered IT governance, IT governance for blockchain technology, IT governance for cloud computing, IT governance for Internet of Things (IoT) devices, IT governance for cybersecurity and data privacy, IT governance for remote and distributed teams, IT governance for agile and DevOps methodologies, and IT governance for digital transformation initiatives. By focusing on these specific areas, the subchapter will provide practical insights and strategies for addressing data privacy regulations in each niche.

The content will emphasize the importance of understanding and complying with data privacy regulations such as the General Data Protection Regulation (GDPR) and the California Consumer Privacy Act (CCPA). It will explore the potential impact of emerging technologies such as AI, blockchain, and IoT on data privacy and discuss how organizations can navigate the complexities of these technologies while ensuring compliance.

Furthermore, the subchapter will provide best practices for implementing robust data privacy frameworks, conducting privacy impact assessments, and establishing effective data governance practices. It will also discuss the role of IT professionals in safeguarding data privacy and the importance of ongoing training and education to stay updated with the evolving regulatory landscape.

By addressing data privacy regulations in IT governance, organizations can build trust with their customers, protect sensitive data, mitigate the risk of data breaches, and ensure compliance with the regulatory requirements. This subchapter will equip CTOs, CEOs, IT professionals, information technology students, technology industry leaders, and computer science students with the knowledge and strategies to address data privacy regulations effectively in the year 2024 and beyond.

Chapter 7: IT Governance for Remote and Distributed Teams

Remote Work Trends in 2024

Remote work has become a prevalent trend in the world of IT governance, and it is expected to continue growing in popularity in 2024. This subchapter will explore the various remote work trends that are expected to shape the IT industry in the coming years.

One of the most significant trends in remote work is the rise of AI-powered IT governance. As artificial intelligence continues to advance, it is being integrated into various aspects of IT governance, including remote work management. AI algorithms can analyze data from remote workers, identify patterns, and provide valuable insights for improving productivity and efficiency. This trend is expected to revolutionize the way IT professionals manage remote teams, enabling them to make data-driven decisions and optimize their operations.

Another trend that will impact remote work in 2024 is the emergence of IT governance for blockchain technology. As blockchain becomes more widely adopted, IT professionals will need to develop governance strategies to ensure the security and integrity of remote work processes involving blockchain. This will involve implementing protocols and standards to protect sensitive data and prevent unauthorized access.

Additionally, IT governance for remote and distributed teams will continue to evolve to meet the needs of an increasingly remote workforce. This trend will encompass implementing effective communication and collaboration tools, ensuring secure access to company resources, and establishing clear performance metrics for remote workers. IT professionals will need to develop strategies to manage and monitor remote teams efficiently, ensuring that they remain productive and aligned with the organization's goals.

Furthermore, IT governance for cybersecurity and data privacy will remain a critical consideration for remote work in 2024. With the increasing number of cyber threats and data breaches, IT professionals must implement robust security measures to protect remote workers and sensitive company information. This includes implementing multi-factor authentication, secure VPNs, and regular security audits to identify vulnerabilities and mitigate risks.

The rise of agile and DevOps methodologies will also impact remote work trends in 2024. These methodologies emphasize collaboration, flexibility, and continuous improvement, making them well-suited for remote work environments. IT professionals will need to adapt their governance strategies to support agile and DevOps practices in remote teams, fostering a culture of collaboration and innovation.

Lastly, IT governance for cloud computing and Internet of Things (IoT) devices will be crucial in 2024. With the increasing reliance on cloud-based services and the proliferation of IoT devices, IT professionals must develop governance strategies to ensure the security, scalability, and reliability of remote work infrastructure. This will involve implementing robust cloud security measures, monitoring IoT devices for potential vulnerabilities, and establishing protocols for remote access to sensitive data.

In conclusion, remote work trends in 2024 will be shaped by AI-powered IT governance, blockchain technology, cybersecurity and data privacy, remote team management, agile and DevOps methodologies, and cloud computing and IoT devices. IT professionals, CTOs, CEOs, and technology industry leaders must stay abreast of these trends and adapt their governance strategies to optimize remote work productivity, security, and collaboration. Likewise, information technology and computer science students should be prepared to enter a workforce that increasingly relies on remote work, and they must acquire the necessary skills and knowledge to succeed in this evolving landscape.

Managing IT Governance for Remote and Distributed Teams

In the ever-evolving digital landscape of 2024, the concept of remote and distributed teams has become the new norm. With advancements in technology and the rise of globalization, organizations are increasingly embracing the benefits of having teams spread across different geographical locations. However, managing IT governance in this context poses unique challenges that require careful consideration and strategic planning.

One of the key aspects of managing IT governance for remote and distributed teams is ensuring effective communication and collaboration. With team members located in different time zones and possibly speaking different languages, it is crucial to establish clear communication channels and protocols. This includes leveraging AI-powered IT governance tools that can facilitate real-time collaboration, automate workflows, and provide insights into team performance.

Moreover, IT governance for remote and distributed teams must also address the specific challenges posed by emerging technologies such as blockchain, cloud computing, and the Internet of Things (IoT). These technologies bring about new complexities in terms of data management, security, and compliance. IT professionals and leaders must ensure that proper governance frameworks are in place to mitigate risks and ensure the smooth operation of these technologies.

Furthermore, cybersecurity and data privacy are paramount concerns when managing IT governance for remote and distributed teams. With team members accessing sensitive information from various locations, it is crucial to implement robust security measures and protocols. This includes regular training on cybersecurity best practices, implementing multi-factor authentication, and conducting regular audits to identify and address vulnerabilities.

Additionally, managing IT governance for remote and distributed teams should also encompass the adoption of agile and DevOps methodologies. These methodologies promote collaboration, flexibility, and continuous improvement, which are essential for the success of distributed teams. IT professionals and leaders should embrace tools and practices that enable seamless integration, automated testing, and continuous deployment.

Lastly, IT governance for remote and distributed teams must align with digital transformation initiatives. As organizations undergo digital transformations to stay competitive, IT governance must support these initiatives by providing the necessary frameworks and guidelines. This includes ensuring proper change management, evaluating the impact of new technologies on existing processes, and fostering a culture of innovation and adaptability.

In conclusion, managing IT governance for remote and distributed teams requires a holistic approach that addresses the unique challenges posed by emerging technologies, cybersecurity risks, and the need for effective communication and collaboration. By leveraging AI-powered tools, embracing agile and DevOps methodologies, and aligning with digital transformation initiatives, organizations can successfully navigate the complexities of remote and distributed teams in the ever-changing landscape of 2024.

Tools and Strategies for Effective IT Governance in Remote Work Environments

In recent years, the rapid advancement of technology and the increasing demand for remote work have transformed the way businesses operate. As organizations embrace this new work paradigm, it is crucial to establish effective IT governance practices to ensure seamless operations, enhanced productivity, and robust cybersecurity. This subchapter explores the tools and strategies that are essential for successful IT governance in remote work environments, keeping in mind the specific needs and challenges of the future IT landscape.

One of the key tools for effective IT governance in remote work environments is AI-powered technology. AI can automate routine tasks, analyze large volumes of data, and provide valuable insights, empowering organizations to make informed decisions and optimize their IT governance processes. AI-powered tools can assist in monitoring and managing remote teams, tracking their performance and productivity, and identifying potential bottlenecks or issues that may arise.

Another important aspect of IT governance in remote work environments is ensuring robust cybersecurity and data privacy. With the rise in cyber threats, organizations need to adopt advanced tools and strategies to protect their sensitive information. This includes implementing multi-factor authentication, encrypted communication channels, and regularly updating security protocols. Additionally, organizations must educate their remote workforce on best practices for cybersecurity and provide access to tools for secure remote access.

Cloud computing has become an integral part of modern IT infrastructure, enabling remote work and collaboration. To effectively govern cloud computing in remote work environments, organizations should establish clear policies and guidelines for cloud usage, ensure data backup and disaster recovery plans are in place, and regularly assess the performance and security of cloud service providers. Utilizing cloud-based project management and collaboration tools can also enhance productivity and enable seamless communication among remote teams.

The Internet of Things (IoT) devices are increasingly being used in remote work environments, providing opportunities for enhanced productivity and connectivity. However, their use also introduces new challenges for IT governance. Organizations must establish policies for secure IoT device usage, conduct regular vulnerability assessments, and implement measures to prevent unauthorized access or data breaches.

Effective IT governance in remote work environments also requires organizations to embrace agile and DevOps methodologies. These methodologies promote collaboration, transparency, and continuous improvement, enabling organizations to adapt quickly to changing circumstances. Embracing agile and DevOps practices can help remote teams work cohesively, deliver projects on time, and ensure high-quality outcomes.

Lastly, IT governance in remote work environments must align with digital transformation initiatives. Organizations should leverage digital tools and technologies to streamline processes, automate workflows, and drive innovation. This includes adopting digital project management tools, leveraging data analytics for decision-making, and embracing emerging technologies such as artificial intelligence and blockchain.

In conclusion, successful IT governance in remote work environments requires the adoption of tools and strategies that address the unique challenges and opportunities of the future IT landscape. From AI-powered technology to robust cybersecurity measures, organizations must leverage these tools to ensure seamless operations, enhanced productivity, and effective collaboration among remote teams. By embracing the digital transformation and aligning IT governance practices with emerging technologies, organizations can thrive in the remote work era of 2024 and beyond.

Chapter 8: IT Governance for Agile

and DevOps Methodologies

The Role of Agile and DevOps in IT Governance

In today's rapidly evolving digital landscape, the role of IT governance has become more critical than ever. As organizations strive to stay ahead of the competition, they must adopt agile and DevOps methodologies to drive innovation and deliver value to their customers. This subchapter explores the role of agile and DevOps in IT governance and how they contribute to the success of organizations in 2024 and beyond.

Agile and DevOps methodologies have revolutionized the way software development and IT operations are approached. Agile emphasizes collaboration, flexibility, and iterative development, while DevOps focuses on streamlining and automating the software delivery process. By combining these two approaches, organizations can achieve faster time to market, improved quality, and increased customer satisfaction.

In the context of IT governance, agile and DevOps methodologies enable organizations to respond quickly to changing business needs and market demands. They provide a framework for effective decision-making, risk management, and resource allocation. By breaking down silos and fostering cross-functional collaboration, agile and DevOps empower CTOs, CEOs, and IT professionals to make informed decisions that align with the organization's strategic goals.

For Information Technology students and computer science students, understanding the role of agile and DevOps in IT governance is crucial for their future careers. As the industry continues to evolve, employers are increasingly seeking professionals who can navigate the complexities of agile and DevOps methodologies and apply them to drive organizational success.

Furthermore, technology industry leaders must embrace agile and DevOps to stay competitive and relevant in an era of digital transformation. With AI-powered IT governance, blockchain technology, cloud computing, Internet of Things (IoT) devices, cybersecurity, data privacy, and remote and distributed teams becoming integral parts of the IT landscape, agile and DevOps provide the foundation for effective governance in these domains.

Finally, agile and DevOps methodologies are essential for organizations embarking on digital transformation initiatives. They enable organizations to adapt quickly to change, experiment with new technologies, and deliver value to customers at a faster pace. By incorporating agile and DevOps into their IT governance strategies, organizations can ensure that their digital transformation initiatives are successful and aligned with their overall business objectives.

In conclusion, the role of agile and DevOps in IT governance cannot be underestimated. They provide the framework for effective decision-making, risk management, and resource allocation in an increasingly complex digital landscape. Whether you are a CTO, CEO, IT professional, Information Technology student, or technology industry leader, understanding and embracing agile and DevOps methodologies is essential for success in IT governance in 2024 and beyond.

Implementing Agile and DevOps Principles in IT Governance Processes

In today's rapidly evolving technological landscape, organizations are constantly seeking ways to enhance their IT governance processes to keep up with the demands of the digital age. This subchapter will delve into the importance of implementing Agile and DevOps principles in IT governance processes, and how these methodologies can drive success in the ever-changing world of technology.

CTOs, CEOs, IT professionals, information technology students, technology industry leaders, and computer science students will find this subchapter invaluable as it explores the future of IT governance in 2024. With the advent of emerging technologies such as AI, blockchain, cloud computing, the Internet of Things (IoT), cybersecurity, data privacy, remote and distributed teams, and digital transformation, the need for agile and DevOps methodologies in IT governance becomes paramount.

Agile and DevOps methodologies promote flexibility, collaboration, and efficiency in IT governance processes. By incorporating Agile principles, organizations can respond quickly to changing requirements and deliver value to their customers in shorter timeframes. DevOps, on the other hand, emphasizes continuous integration, continuous delivery, and collaboration between development and operations teams, resulting in more streamlined and automated processes.

In the context of AI-powered IT governance, Agile and DevOps principles enable organizations to adapt and scale their AI initiatives rapidly. They facilitate the iterative development and deployment of AI models, enabling organizations to harness the power of AI while mitigating risks and ensuring compliance.

Similarly, for blockchain technology, Agile and DevOps methodologies enable organizations to experiment, iterate, and rapidly deploy blockchain solutions. These methodologies help organizations overcome the challenges associated with the complex and decentralized nature of blockchain technology.

Cloud computing, IoT devices, cybersecurity, data privacy, remote and distributed teams, and digital transformation initiatives all benefit from the agility and collaboration brought about by Agile and DevOps methodologies in IT governance. These methodologies allow organizations to adapt to the dynamic nature of these technologies and drive innovation while ensuring security, privacy, and compliance.

In conclusion, the future of IT governance in 2024 lies in the implementation of Agile and DevOps principles. This subchapter will provide valuable insights and strategies for CTOs, CEOs, IT professionals, information technology students, technology industry leaders, and computer science students to navigate the evolving landscape of IT governance and drive success in the digital age.

Overcoming Challenges in Agile and DevOps-based IT Governance

In today's rapidly evolving technological landscape, agile and DevOps methodologies have become essential for organizations striving for innovation and efficiency. However, implementing these approaches in IT governance can present various challenges. This subchapter will delve into the hurdles faced in agile and DevOps-based IT governance and provide strategies for overcoming them.

One of the primary challenges in agile and DevOps-based IT governance is maintaining alignment between business objectives and IT initiatives. Traditional governance models often struggle to keep up with the speed and flexibility required by agile and DevOps practices. To overcome this, organizations must establish clear communication channels between business and IT stakeholders. Regular meetings, shared goals, and ongoing collaboration can help ensure that IT initiatives are aligned with business objectives.

Another challenge lies in managing the complexity that arises from the adoption of emerging technologies. As AI-powered IT governance, blockchain, cloud computing, IoT devices, cybersecurity, data privacy, and digital transformation initiatives become integral parts of organizations' IT infrastructure, governance frameworks must adapt accordingly. This requires establishing robust policies, frameworks, and controls that govern the use of these technologies while ensuring compliance, security, and risk management.

Furthermore, the rise of remote and distributed teams poses unique challenges for agile and DevOps-based IT governance. Collaboration and coordination can be hindered by geographical distances and cultural differences. Organizations must invest in communication tools, virtual collaboration platforms, and training programs to foster effective teamwork and knowledge sharing.

Moreover, the dynamic nature of agile and DevOps methodologies necessitates continuous monitoring and improvement. Organizations must embrace a culture of learning and adaptability, encouraging IT professionals to experiment, learn from failures, and continuously refine their processes. Establishing metrics and key performance indicators (KPIs) can provide insights into the effectiveness of IT governance practices and facilitate continuous improvement.

In conclusion, agile and DevOps-based IT governance present both opportunities and challenges for organizations. By addressing the alignment between business objectives and IT initiatives, managing the complexity of emerging technologies, fostering collaboration in remote and distributed teams, and embracing a culture of learning and improvement, organizations can overcome these challenges and successfully implement agile and

DevOps-based IT governance. This will enable them to navigate the ever-changing technological landscape and drive innovation and efficiency in the future of IT governance in 2024 and beyond.

Chapter 9: IT Governance for Digital Transformation Initiatives

The Significance of Digital Transformation in 2024

In the fast-paced digital era we live in, the significance of digital transformation cannot be overstated. As we approach the year 2024, the need for organizations to embrace digital transformation has become more critical than ever before. This subchapter will delve into the various aspects of digital transformation and its importance in shaping the future of IT governance.

For CTOs, CEOs, and IT professionals, understanding the significance of digital transformation is crucial for staying ahead in the rapidly evolving technology landscape. Digital transformation involves leveraging technology to fundamentally change the way businesses operate, enabling them to be more efficient, agile, and customer-centric. It encompasses the adoption of emerging technologies such as artificial intelligence (AI), blockchain, cloud computing, and the Internet of Things (IoT). By embracing digital transformation, organizations can gain a competitive edge, increase productivity, and drive innovation.

IT governance in 2024 will heavily rely on AI-powered solutions. AI has the potential to revolutionize IT governance by automating processes, enhancing decision-making, and improving overall efficiency. Organizations that successfully integrate AI-powered IT governance will be able to harness the power of data and make informed decisions in real-time.

Furthermore, the subchapter will explore how digital transformation impacts IT governance in specific domains. It will delve into the unique challenges and opportunities in IT governance for blockchain technology, cloud computing, IoT devices, cybersecurity, data privacy, remote and distributed teams, agile and DevOps methodologies, and digital transformation initiatives.

For technology industry leaders and computer science students, this subchapter will provide valuable insights into the future of IT governance. It will highlight the emerging trends, best practices, and strategies for success in managing IT governance in the era of digital transformation.

Information technology students will find this subchapter particularly relevant as it will equip them with the knowledge and skills necessary to navigate the evolving IT landscape. It will provide them with a roadmap for understanding the significance of digital transformation and its impact on IT governance.

In conclusion, the significance of digital transformation in 2024 cannot be ignored. It is a transformative force that is reshaping the future of IT governance. CTOs, CEOs, IT professionals, information technology students, technology industry leaders, and computer science students must recognize its importance and proactively embrace digital transformation to ensure success in the ever-changing digital landscape. By doing so, organizations can position themselves as leaders in their respective niches and thrive in the digital age.

Aligning IT Governance with Digital Transformation Strategies

In today's rapidly evolving digital landscape, organizations are increasingly relying on digital transformation initiatives to stay competitive and meet the ever-changing needs of their customers. However, implementing these transformative strategies requires a strong foundation of IT governance to ensure the effective and efficient use of technology resources. In this subchapter, we will explore the importance of aligning IT governance with digital transformation strategies and discuss key considerations for CTOs, CEOs, IT professionals, information technology students, technology industry leaders, and computer science students.

IT governance in 2024 is no longer a separate entity from digital transformation. Instead, it has become an integral part of the process, enabling organizations to effectively manage risks, optimize resource allocation, and ensure alignment between IT and business objectives. By aligning IT governance with digital transformation strategies, organizations can ensure that their investments in technology yield the desired outcomes and drive business value.

One of the emerging trends in IT governance is the use of AI-powered solutions. AI can enhance decision-making processes, automate routine tasks, and provide real-time insights into the organization's IT landscape. By leveraging AI-powered IT governance tools, organizations can better manage their digital transformation initiatives, identify potential risks, and make data-driven decisions.

Another area of focus is IT governance for blockchain technology, cloud computing, and Internet of Things (IoT) devices. As these technologies continue to disrupt traditional business models, organizations need to establish governance frameworks that address their unique risks and challenges. This includes ensuring the security and integrity of blockchain transactions, managing the complexities of cloud computing environments, and addressing privacy concerns associated with IoT devices.

Additionally, IT governance for cybersecurity and data privacy is crucial in the digital age. With the increasing frequency and sophistication of cyber threats, organizations must implement robust governance practices to protect their sensitive data and ensure compliance with regulatory requirements. This involves establishing clear policies, implementing security controls, and regularly assessing and monitoring the organization's cybersecurity posture.

Furthermore, IT governance for remote and distributed teams and for agile and DevOps methodologies is vital for organizations embracing flexible work arrangements and agile development practices. Effective governance in these contexts requires clear communication channels, collaboration tools, and streamlined decision-making processes to ensure alignment and accountability.

Lastly, IT governance plays a critical role in supporting digital transformation initiatives. By setting clear goals, defining roles and responsibilities, and establishing metrics for success, organizations can navigate the complexities of digital transformation and drive innovation.

In conclusion, aligning IT governance with digital transformation strategies is essential for organizations to succeed in the digital era. The subchapter has explored various aspects of IT governance in the context of digital transformation, including AI-powered solutions, blockchain technology, cloud computing, IoT devices, cybersecurity, remote teams, agile methodologies, and digital transformation initiatives. By understanding and implementing effective IT governance practices, CTOs, CEOs, IT professionals, information technology students, technology industry leaders, and computer science students can position their organizations for success in the dynamic digital landscape of 2024 and beyond.

Leveraging Technology for Successful Digital Transformation

In today's rapidly evolving digital landscape, successful organizations understand the importance of leveraging technology for digital transformation. It is no longer a question of if, but rather when and how to implement digital initiatives to stay competitive and relevant in the market. In this subchapter, we will explore various aspects of leveraging technology for successful digital transformation, focusing on the key areas of IT governance in 2024, AI-powered IT governance, IT governance for blockchain technology, IT governance for cloud computing, IT governance for Internet of Things (IoT) devices, IT governance for cybersecurity and data privacy, IT governance for remote and distributed teams, IT governance for agile and DevOps methodologies, and IT governance for digital transformation initiatives.

As CTOs, CEOs, IT professionals, information technology students, technology industry leaders, and computer science students, it is crucial to understand the role of technology in driving digital transformation. Technology acts as an enabler, providing the necessary tools and infrastructure to support digital initiatives. However, successful digital transformation goes beyond technology implementation; it requires a strategic and holistic approach.

AI-powered IT governance is a game-changer in the digital era. By harnessing the power of artificial intelligence and machine learning, organizations can automate and optimize IT governance processes, resulting in improved decision-making, increased efficiency, and reduced risk. AI-powered IT governance empowers organizations to make data-driven decisions, anticipate future challenges, and stay ahead of the competition.

When it comes to blockchain technology, IT governance plays a vital role in ensuring its successful implementation. Blockchain offers decentralized and transparent systems, but it also brings unique challenges in terms of governance, security, and compliance. Organizations must establish robust IT governance frameworks to address these challenges and leverage the potential of blockchain technology.

Cloud computing has revolutionized the IT landscape, enabling organizations to scale, innovate, and transform their operations. However, cloud adoption also brings governance challenges, such as data privacy, security, and compliance. Effective IT governance for cloud computing involves establishing clear policies, procedures, and controls to ensure data protection, vendor management, and regulatory compliance.

The proliferation of IoT devices has created new opportunities and challenges for organizations. IT governance for IoT devices involves managing a diverse and interconnected ecosystem, ensuring data integrity, privacy, and security. Organizations must implement robust IT governance frameworks that address the unique risks associated with IoT devices and leverage their potential for digital transformation.

In an era of increasing cyber threats and data privacy concerns, IT governance plays a critical role in safeguarding organizational assets. Effective governance frameworks for cybersecurity and data privacy involve proactive risk management, continuous monitoring, and compliance with regulatory requirements. Organizations must prioritize IT governance for cybersecurity and data privacy to protect their valuable assets and maintain customer trust.

The rise of remote and distributed teams has become a norm in today's digital workplace. IT governance for remote and distributed teams involves establishing clear communication channels, collaboration tools, and performance metrics. Organizations must adapt their IT governance frameworks to support remote work environments and ensure effective teamwork, productivity, and accountability.

Agile and DevOps methodologies have emerged as key drivers of digital transformation. Effective IT governance for agile and DevOps involves aligning business objectives with IT initiatives, promoting collaboration, and ensuring continuous improvement. Organizations must adopt agile IT governance practices to enable faster time to market, increased innovation, and enhanced customer satisfaction.

Digital transformation initiatives require a comprehensive IT governance strategy that encompasses all aspects of technology adoption and implementation. IT governance for digital transformation involves setting clear goals, defining governance structures, establishing performance metrics, and continuously monitoring and adapting to changing market dynamics. Organizations must embrace digital transformation as a journey and leverage technology strategically to drive innovation and business growth.

In conclusion, leveraging technology for successful digital transformation is essential for organizations in the rapidly evolving digital landscape. As CTOs, CEOs, IT professionals, information technology students, technology industry leaders, and computer science students, understanding the role of technology in driving digital transformation and adopting effective IT governance practices is crucial for long-term success. By embracing AI-powered IT governance, addressing the unique governance challenges of blockchain technology, cloud computing, IoT devices, cybersecurity, and data privacy, remote and distributed teams, agile and DevOps methodologies, and digital transformation initiatives, organizations can drive innovation, gain a competitive edge, and thrive in the digital era.

Chapter 10: Conclusion: Strategies for Success in IT Governance

Recap of Key IT Governance Topics

In this subchapter, we will provide a comprehensive recap of the key IT governance topics discussed throughout this book, "The Future of IT Governance in 2024: Strategies for Success." As technology continues to evolve rapidly, it becomes increasingly crucial for organizations to effectively manage their IT systems and ensure the alignment of IT with business goals. This recap will serve as a useful summary for CTOs, CEOs, IT professionals, information technology students, technology industry leaders, computer science students, and anyone interested in the field of IT governance.

IT Governance in 2024: As technology landscapes continue to evolve, IT governance has become more complex. In this book, we have explored various strategies and frameworks to adapt to these changes and ensure effective decision-making and accountability in IT.

AI-Powered IT Governance: Artificial Intelligence has emerged as a game-changer in IT governance. We have discussed how AI can be leveraged to enhance decision-making, automate governance processes, and improve risk management.

IT Governance for Blockchain Technology: Blockchain technology offers opportunities for increased transparency, security, and trust in IT governance. We have delved into the challenges and best practices for governing blockchain technology effectively.

IT Governance for Cloud Computing: The widespread adoption of cloud computing has necessitated the development of robust IT governance frameworks. We have explored the unique challenges and strategies for governing cloud-based systems securely and efficiently.

IT Governance for Internet of Things (IoT) Devices: With the proliferation of IoT devices, organizations must establish governance mechanisms to ensure data privacy, security, and compliance. We have examined the key considerations and frameworks for governing IoT devices effectively.

IT Governance for Cybersecurity and Data Privacy: Cybersecurity and data privacy are critical concerns for organizations in the digital age. We have discussed the importance of integrating cybersecurity and data privacy into IT governance frameworks to mitigate risks effectively.

IT Governance for Remote and Distributed Teams: The rise of remote and distributed teams has necessitated the development of governance strategies tailored to this new work environment. We have explored the challenges and best practices for governing remote teams successfully.

IT Governance for Agile and DevOps Methodologies: Agile and DevOps methodologies have revolutionized software development practices. We have examined how to integrate these methodologies into IT governance frameworks to foster innovation, collaboration, and speed to market.

IT Governance for Digital Transformation Initiatives: Digital transformation initiatives require robust IT governance frameworks to ensure successful outcomes. We have explored the key considerations and strategies for governing digital transformation effectively.

This recap provides a snapshot of the critical IT governance topics covered in this book. By understanding and implementing these strategies, CTOs, CEOs, IT professionals, information technology students, technology industry leaders, and computer science students can navigate the complex IT landscape of 2024 and beyond, driving organizational success in the digital age.

Best Practices for Successful IT Governance in 2024

Introduction:

In the rapidly evolving landscape of technology, successful IT governance is crucial for organizations to effectively manage their information technology resources, mitigate risks, and achieve strategic objectives. As we venture into 2024, there are several emerging trends and challenges that CTOs, CEOs, IT professionals, information technology students, technology industry leaders, and computer science students should be aware of. This subchapter explores the best practices for successful IT governance in 2024, focusing on various niches such as AI-powered IT governance, IT governance for blockchain technology, cloud computing, Internet of Things (IoT) devices, cybersecurity and data privacy, remote and distributed teams, agile and DevOps methodologies, and digital transformation initiatives.

1. Embrace AI-powered IT Governance:

With the advent of artificial intelligence (AI), organizations must leverage AI-powered IT governance tools to enhance decision-making processes, automate repetitive tasks, and improve overall efficiency. By harnessing the power of AI, CTOs and IT professionals can streamline IT governance processes, analyze vast amounts of data, and identify potential risks and opportunities in real-time.

2. Adopt Blockchain Technology:

Blockchain technology has emerged as a game-changer in various industries. In 2024, organizations should consider implementing blockchain-based IT governance frameworks to enhance transparency, security, and accountability. By leveraging blockchain, organizations can ensure the integrity of their IT assets, streamline audit processes, and establish trust among stakeholders.

3. Secure Cloud Computing:

As cloud computing continues to be a vital component of modern IT infrastructure, organizations must prioritize robust IT governance practices specific to the cloud. This includes implementing stringent access controls, data encryption, regular audits, and comprehensive risk management strategies to protect sensitive information and mitigate potential breaches.

4. Strengthen IoT Governance:

With the proliferation of IoT devices, organizations must establish effective IT governance practices to manage and secure these connected devices. This involves implementing IoT-specific policies, ensuring data privacy, conducting regular vulnerability assessments, and establishing clear guidelines for IoT device usage.

5. Prioritize Cybersecurity and Data Privacy:

In an increasingly digital world, cybersecurity and data privacy are paramount. Organizations should adopt comprehensive IT governance frameworks that encompass robust cybersecurity measures, regular security assessments, employee training, incident response plans, and compliance with data protection regulations.

6. Manage Remote and Distributed Teams:

With the rise of remote work, organizations should adapt their IT governance practices to effectively manage and support distributed teams. This includes implementing collaboration tools, ensuring secure remote access, providing adequate training and resources, and establishing clear communication channels.

7. Embrace Agile and DevOps Methodologies:

To stay competitive in the digital landscape, organizations should adopt agile and DevOps methodologies, which require agile IT governance practices. This involves breaking down silos, fostering collaboration, enabling continuous integration and deployment, and empowering cross-functional teams.

8. Drive Digital Transformation Initiatives:

Successful IT governance in 2024 requires organizations to embrace digital transformation initiatives. This involves aligning IT strategies with business objectives, establishing clear governance structures, fostering innovation, and continuously evaluating and adapting IT governance practices to support evolving technologies.

Conclusion:

In 2024, successful IT governance requires organizations to embrace emerging technologies, adapt to new challenges, and implement best practices across various niches. By leveraging AI-powered tools, embracing blockchain technology, securing cloud computing, managing IoT devices, prioritizing cybersecurity, empowering remote teams, adopting agile methodologies, and driving digital transformation initiatives, organizations can position themselves for success in the ever-evolving IT landscape. CTOs, CEOs, IT professionals, information technology students, technology industry leaders, and computer science students must stay abreast of these best practices to effectively navigate the IT governance landscape in 2024 and beyond.

Future Trends and Predictions for IT Governance

As we look towards the future, it is clear that IT governance will continue to evolve and adapt to the rapidly changing technological landscape. In this subchapter, we will explore some of the key trends and predictions for IT governance in the coming years.

One of the most exciting developments in IT governance is the rise of AI-powered systems. Artificial Intelligence (AI) has the potential to greatly enhance the efficiency and effectiveness of IT governance processes. By leveraging AI algorithms and machine learning capabilities, organizations can automate decision-making, risk assessment, and compliance monitoring. This will enable CTOs, CEOs, and IT professionals to focus on strategic activities, while AI-powered systems handle routine governance tasks.

Another area of significant growth is IT governance for blockchain technology. Blockchain has emerged as a disruptive force across various industries, and IT governance frameworks will need to adapt to incorporate its unique characteristics. Blockchain offers enhanced transparency, security, and decentralization, but it also presents new challenges in terms of governance and compliance. Organizations will need to develop specific governance strategies to address these challenges and ensure the successful adoption and implementation of blockchain technology.

Cloud computing is another trend that will shape the future of IT governance. As more organizations migrate their infrastructure and services to the cloud, effective governance will become crucial. IT governance frameworks will need to address issues such as data security, privacy, and vendor management in the context of cloud computing. Additionally, organizations will need to establish robust controls and processes to ensure compliance with relevant regulations and standards.

The proliferation of Internet of Things (IoT) devices presents both opportunities and challenges for IT governance. As the number of connected devices continues to grow, organizations will need to implement governance frameworks that address the unique risks associated with IoT devices. This includes ensuring the security and privacy of data transmitted and stored by these devices, as well as managing the complexity of an increasingly interconnected ecosystem.

Cybersecurity and data privacy will remain a top priority for IT governance in the future. With the increasing frequency and sophistication of cyber threats, organizations must implement robust governance frameworks to protect their data and systems. This includes proactive risk assessment, incident response planning, and continuous monitoring to detect and mitigate potential threats.

The rise of remote and distributed teams, as well as the adoption of agile and DevOps methodologies, will also impact IT governance. Organizations will need to develop governance frameworks that support collaboration and effective decision-making in distributed environments. This includes establishing clear roles and responsibilities, implementing communication and collaboration tools, and ensuring compliance with governance policies and standards.

Lastly, digital transformation initiatives will drive the need for effective IT governance. As organizations embrace digital technologies to enhance their operations and customer experiences, governance frameworks will need to address the unique challenges of these initiatives. This includes ensuring alignment with business objectives, managing risks associated with technology adoption, and monitoring the impact of digital transformation on governance processes.

In conclusion, the future of IT governance holds exciting opportunities and challenges. From AI-powered systems to blockchain technology, cloud computing, IoT devices, cybersecurity, remote teams, agile methodologies, and digital transformation initiatives, IT governance will play a crucial role in enabling organizations to navigate the evolving technological landscape. By staying ahead of these trends and adopting proactive governance strategies, CTOs, CEOs, IT professionals, and technology industry leaders can ensure the success of their organizations in the digital age.

www.ingramcontent.com/pod-product-compliance
Lightning Source LLC
LaVergne TN
LVHW051615050326
832903LV00033B/4507